AMERICAN CARS
THROUGH THE DECADES

American Cars
before 1950

Craig Cheetham

GARETH**STEVENS**
GS
PUBLISHING
A Member of the WRC Media Family of Companies

Please visit our web site at: www.garethstevens.com
For a free color catalog describing Gareth Stevens Publishing's
list of high-quality books and multimedia programs,
call 1-800-542-2595 (USA) or 1-800-387-3178 (Canada).
Gareth Stevens Publishing's fax: (414) 332-3567.

Library of Congress Cataloging-in-Publication Data

Cheetham, Craig.
    American cars before 1950 / Craig Cheetham.
        p. cm. — (American cars through the decades)
    Includes bibliographical references and index.
    ISBN-13: 978-0-8368-7723-6 (lib. bdg.)
    1. Automobiles—United States—History. I. Title.
    TL23.C44   2007
    629.2220973'09041—dc22   2006051066

This North American edition first published in 2007 by
Gareth Stevens Publishing
A Member of the WRC Media Family of Companies
330 West Olive Street, Suite 100
Milwaukee, WI 53212 USA

Copyright © 2007 Amber Books Ltd

Produced by Amber Books Ltd., Bradley's Close,
74–77 White Lion Street, London N1 9PF, U.K.

Project Editor: Michael Spilling
Design: Joe Conneally

Gareth Stevens managing editor: Valerie J. Weber
Gareth Stevens editor: Alan Wachtel
Gareth Stevens art direction: Tammy West
Gareth Stevens cover design: Dave Kowalski
Gareth Stevens production: Jessica Yanke and Robert Kraus

Illustrations and photographs copyright International Masters
Publishers AB/Aerospace–Art-Tech

Printed in the United States of America

1 2 3 4 5 6 7 8 9 10 10 09 08 07 06

Table of Contents

Auburn Speedster

With its elegant looks and high price, the Auburn Speedster was a car for only the richest people.

Auburn Speedsters had a **supercharger** — a pump that forced extra air into the engine. This enabled the engine to send extra power to the wheels, making them turn faster.

The Speedster had Auburn's logo — a winged figure — on the side.

Drivers could store baggage in a hatch behind the seats. The hatch was big enough for a set of golf clubs.

The Speedster featured **drum brakes** that had more stopping power than other car brakes of the time.

The steering wheel was on the right-hand side in the Speedster. This was so the driver could step off the sidewalk and into the driver's seat.

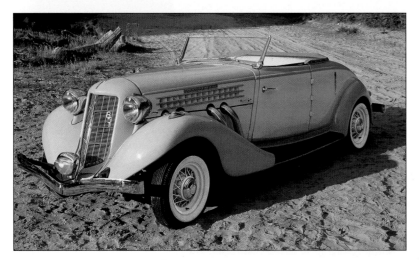

The most popular Speedster was the **convertible**, with its folding top and leather upholstery.

1928

Auburn launches the first Speedster "Boat-tail." It was called this because its rear end looked like the front of a boat.

1935

Auburn launches the Speedster 851 (left), which had a rounder front end and a powerful 160-**horsepower** engine.

Auburn launched the Speedster in 1928. The company wanted the car to appeal to the wealthy. It was a regular sight in Hollywood, California, where movie stars worked. It was an advanced car for its time, with powerful brakes and an eight-**cylinder** engine. The Speedster was the first U.S. car that was able to maintain speeds of 100 miles (161 kilometers) per hour for more than twelve hours. In part, its speed was a result of the car's **aerodynamic** shape.

Fewer than 2,000 Speedsters were built — all of them by hand. Road testers said that the car performed well, especially when going around corners. Today, it is an American legend and is very popular with car collectors. Speedsters often sell for more than $1 million.

UNDER THE SKIN

The Speedster had large, powerful drum brakes, which were good at slowing down the heavy car.

5

Chrysler Airflow

The Chrysler Airflow looked unusual because it was designed by aircraft engineers who wanted it to cut through the air as smoothly as possible.

The car's aerodynamic lines helped it go fast by reducing **wind resistance**. This also meant it used less fuel.

The car's eight-cylinder engine was mounted far forward.

The Airflow did not have a normal **chassis**. Instead, the body was wrapped around a steel frame for extra strength. Chrysler used aircraft-building methods to create it.

Chrysler said the Airflow's tires were "puncture proof." Each tire had two tubes inside, so even if the first tube burst, the second one stayed inflated.

The Airflow's radiator **grille** was built into the curve of the hood for a smoother look. People said it looked like a waterfall.

6

Most Airflows have split windshields, like the one on this car. Some later models had a curved glass design.

1934

The Airflow appears for the first time. It is available in long and short body styles.

1937

After just three years, Chrysler stops production of the Airflow. The company sold only 4,600 in 1937 — one-tenth of what it hoped to sell.

Chrysler's Airflow was a big step forward for the car industry. When designing the car, Chrysler used a **wind tunnel** to see how wind resistance slowed the car down. Today, all car manufacturers use a wind tunnel when designing new cars.

Expensive but Popular

The Airflow set speed records, and its **transmission** was much quieter than those in other cars of the time. The methods Chrysler used to build it, however, made it expensive, and its unusual looks did not appeal to many car buyers. As a result, the Airflow did not sell well, and Chrysler lost a lot of money.

UNDER THE SKIN

The Airflow's body panels were mounted on a steel-tube frame that was much like the structure of modern cars.

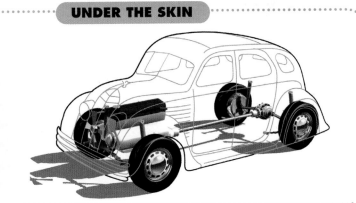

7

Cord 810

When it first appeared, people said the Cord 810 was the most advanced car in the world.

The Cord was the first car to have pop-up headlights.

The car's front and rear side windows were the same size and shape.

Many people called the Cord the "coffin-nose" because of the shape of its hood.

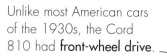

Most Cords were four-door **sedans**. The car was also available as a **coupe** and a convertible.

Unlike most American cars of the 1930s, the Cord 810 had **front-wheel drive**.

The pop-up lights on the Cord 810's front fenders were based on aircraft landing lights.

1935

Cord launches the 810, and it receives many great reviews.

1938

Money problems force the Cord Corporation to close because it could not raise money for new models.

The Cord 810 could have been one of the most successful cars ever made. It was certainly a car of the future, because it had front-wheel drive and pop-up headlights long before any other car. Its engine was also very quiet, even at high speeds. The Cord Corporation, however, had serious financial problems.

comfortable. It was expensive to build and sell, however, so most people could not afford it. After three years, the company collapsed, and that was the end of the Cord.

Expensive Style

The Cord's aerodynamic styling was only part of its appeal, because it was also

UNDER THE SKIN

The Cord had a 289-cubic inch (4,736-cubic centimeter) V-8 engine that was built by an aircraft maker.

Duesenberg SJ

In the 1930s, the Duesenberg was one of the world's finest cars. It was built to be as light and powerful as possible.

The car's eight-cylinder engine had a supercharger that gave it a huge output of 320 horsepower — more than its rivals.

The SJ's air-assisted brakes were huge and operated on all four wheels.

The dashboard on the Duesenberg was made out of lightweight aluminum, instead of steel, to make the car lighter.

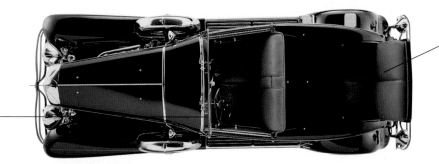

An extra pair of passenger seats folded out of the SJ's body at the car's back.

The grand, sweeping shape of the Duesenberg SJ made it special. It was truly enormous, making most cars on the road look tiny by comparison.

Today, when people talk about **supercars**, they probably mean the Mercedes-McLaren SLR or the Ferrari Enzo. The Duesenberg SJ was the supercar of its day. Everybody wanted to drive an SJ, but only rich people could afford one.

Handmade Supercar

Every part of the SJ was handmade. The company used light aluminum instead of steel where possible to keep the car's weight down. The car was so fast and powerful that, in 1935, American racecar driver A. B. Jenkins averaged 135 miles (217 km) per hour over a twenty-four hour drive at Bonneville, Utah. His fastest lap was more than 160 miles (257 km) per hour.

The SJ was very popular with movie stars. Hollywood legends Gary Cooper and Clark Gable both owned one.

1928

Duesenberg launches the stunning Model J, which becomes the most desirable car for many Americans. The SJ came later and was even fancier.

1932

Duesenberg founder Fred Duesenberg crashes an SJ while testing it at high speed and dies.

UNDER THE SKIN

Duesenberg's hand-built engines were modern in their design. The supercharger gave the engine power to rival many modern performance cars.

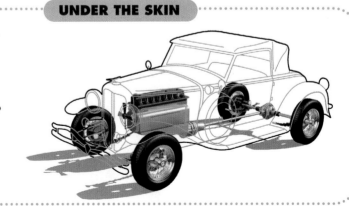

Ford Model T

The Model T was not much to look at, but it is the car that made driving affordable to large numbers of people.

Model Ts had no windshield wipers. Instead, they had a flap in the windshield that opened, letting the driver see out in the rain.

The engine was so reliable that when Model Ts reached the end of their lives, many farmers removed their engines to use in farm machinery.

Model T drivers had to turn a crank to start the car's engine.

Drivers had to pull cables connected to the car's rear wheels to work the brakes. Model T brakes were not very good. Most Model T drivers slowed the car using its gears.

Although the car came in other colors, many believe Henry Ford once said, "You can have any color as long as it's black." Ford used black because it was the cheapest paint, and he wanted to sell cars for the lowest price possible.

making cars very quickly. As a result, new cars became much cheaper than ever before. By 1927, Ford Motor Company was one of the biggest companies in the world, and many people were driving cars.

Henry Ford was the son of an Irish potato farmer who came to the United States to work in the farming industry. Henry turned his back on farming and became the man who put the world on wheels. He built his first car in 1903 so that he could race it. Later, he founded a company dedicated to building reliable cars that most ordinary people could afford.

Some businessmen backed his company, and Ford started making the Model T in 1908. Using new manufacturing methods, Ford began

1908

Ford's first Model T rolls off the assembly line in Dearborn, Michigan, on October 1. By the end of the year, Ford has built 395.

1927

The Model T is replaced with the Model A. By this time, Ford had sold more than fifteen million Model Ts around the world.

UNDER THE SKIN

Part of the Model T's appeal was its simple layout. Its big engine produced only 20 horsepower, but it was never under strain. Some lasted for years without needing repairs.

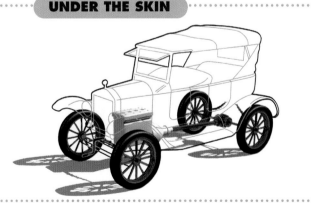

Ford Model A

The Model T was such a huge success for Ford that, by the mid-1920s, other car companies were building similar cars. Ford's answer was the more powerful Model A.

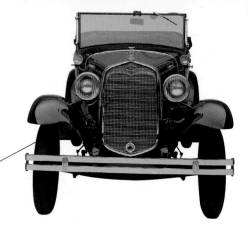

The all-new, four-cylinder engine had twice the power of the Model T. It also had an electric starter, so there was no need for a starting crank.

With its curvier front and its larger body, the Model A looked more modern than the Model T.

Most Model A cars had more space for passengers than the old Model Ts. The Model A came in more than twenty different body styles — from two-seat racers to delivery vans.

Unlike the Model T, the Model A had drum brakes that slowed all four wheels.

The rounder, smoother nose of the Model A made it look much more modern than the Model T.

1927

Ford introduces the Model A. More than ten million people visit Ford dealers to see the car during its first week on sale.

1932

Ford stops producing the Model A in the United States and concentrates on its V-8-powered range instead. In Britain, the Model A remains on sale until 1937.

A fter nineteen years and sales of more than fifteen million cars, the popularity of the Ford Model T was coming to an end in the United States. Other car makers offered more advanced and more comfortable cars. Ford fought back with the Model A.

In the United States, the Model A remained in production for only five years — but nearly three million were sold. The Model A was also built in Britain. It was produced for ten years there.

Low-cost Master

The company used the Model T's low-cost production line. The Model A was more comfortable and faster than the Model T, with a top speed of 65 miles (105 km) per hour.

UNDER THE SKIN

The Model A's biggest advance was its four-wheel drum brakes. They were much more effective than the brakes on the Model T.

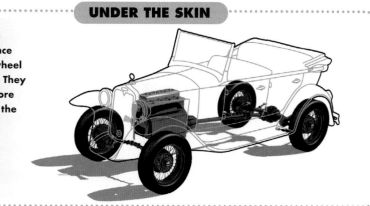

Ford Coupe 1934

Ford started another chapter in the history of American cars with the first V-8 engine to appear in a car sold in a showroom.

The Coupe was the first car to have three windows and a windshield. This style set a trend that was copied by many other car makers.

Ford's small-block V-8 engine had two rows of four cylinders side-by-side in a V-shape. This design made the engine much smaller than many earlier engines. It could be set to different power levels.

The trunk of the Ford Coupe was smaller than it looked. Most of the space in the car's rear end was taken up by the rear **axle**.

The car's front and rear bumpers had springs behind them. If the car had a low-speed collision, its bumpers would spring back with no damage.

The front tires of the Coupe are narrower than those at the rear — a design that is also typical of hot rods.

1932

Ford introduces the first car with a V-8 engine. The Ford line-up of models is now speedy, simple to maintain, and cheap.

1935

Henry Ford receives a letter from bandits Bonnie and Clyde, complimenting him on building fast and reliable cars. The Coupe was the perfect getaway car, they said.

Coupe was one of the most stylish cars on the market because of its short, curvy body.

In fact, the Coupe became popular in the 1940s and 1950s with the first builders of **hot rods**. The V-8 engine was easy to modify to give the car extra power.

American cars were famous for their V-8 engines. The design enables car makers to fit a large-**capacity** engine — 244-cubic-inch (3,998-cc) or more — into a space that normally fit only a smaller engine with four cylinders. The V-8's design enabled companies to produce smaller cars.

First V-8

Ford built the first American mass-produced V-8, beating Chevrolet by two years. To show how powerful a small engine could be, Ford created the Coupe. At the time, many people thought the

UNDER THE SKIN

The engine was advanced, but the rest of the Coupe was simple, with a normal chassis and rear wheel drive.

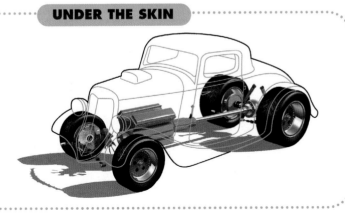

Graham Hollywood

After the Cord Corporation went out of business, Graham-Paige tried to give its design new life with the Graham Hollywood.

The Hollywood's split windshield gave it the look of a fighter airplane.

Under the hood, the Hollywood had a supercharged six-cylinder engine.

The car's headlights were mounted in small pods on top of the front fenders.

From the side, the Hollywood looked like the Cord 810. The doors, roofs, and fenders were the same.

The body style of the Graham Hollywood was based on the Cord 810, but the front end was different.

1939

Graham-Paige launches the Graham Hollywood, but sales are slow.

1940

Graham stops production of the Hollywood after losing a lot of money.

After Cord went out of business in 1938, the small car maker Graham-Paige approached the owners of the design for permission to put it back into production. The owners agreed, enabling Graham-Paige to build its own version.

Graham Hollywoods were built. Like the Cord Corporation, Graham-Paige lost money on the project and was forced to stop production in 1940, after just two years.

New Cord

The new version used most of the Cord's body parts, but it had a simpler **rear-wheel drive** layout and fixed headlights.

The car was still very expensive to make, however, and its unusual looks did not help sales. Fewer than 1,000

UNDER THE SKIN

To convert the Cord design to rear wheel drive, Graham-Paige had to design a new chassis for the car.

Hudson Terraplane

The Hudson Terraplane was built to be cheaper than Fords or Chevrolets but just as good. For this reason, Hudsons became popular cars.

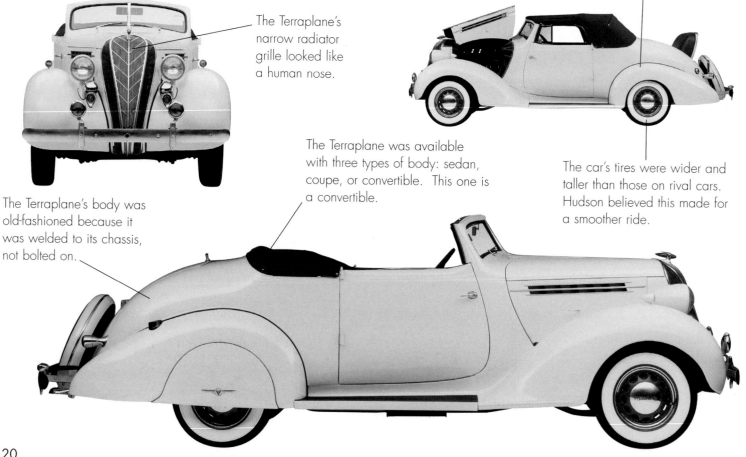

Drivers could remove the covers over the rear wheels to change a tire.

The Terraplane's narrow radiator grille looked like a human nose.

The Terraplane was available with three types of body: sedan, coupe, or convertible. This one is a convertible.

The car's tires were wider and taller than those on rival cars. Hudson believed this made for a smoother ride.

The Terraplane's body was old-fashioned because it was welded to its chassis, not bolted on.

A modern body shape covered an old-fashioned chassis layout on the Hudson Terraplane.

1932

The first Terraplanes go on sale and get very good reviews.

1947

After fifteen years, the Hudson Hornet (above) replaces the Terraplane.

For many years, Ford and Chevrolet were the biggest car makers in the United States. The small company Hudson decided to produce a car to match the Ford Model A. In 1932, the Terraplane first appeared on the road.

New Challenger

The Terraplane had a more rounded body style than its main rivals, and it had more room inside. It was also cheaper, and it rode more smoothly. Hudson, however, did not have as many dealers to sell its cars as Ford or General Motors.

As a result, the Terraplane never sold as well as its main rivals. Even so, it was popular enough to keep Hudson going well into the 1950s.

UNDER THE SKIN

Hudsons were well made, with the body welded to the chassis in thirty places.

Lincoln Zephyr

The Zephyr was Lincoln's smallest car when it first came out. It was also one of the most advanced cars of its time.

The Zephyr was available in three styles: a four-door sedan; a two-door convertible; and, as shown here, a very rare four-door convertible.

The car's power came from a **V-12** engine that produced 110 horsepower. This was not a lot of power, but testers said it was one of the smoothest-running and quietest engines on the market.

The car's rear doors swung toward its back to make it easier for passengers to get in and out.

The Lincoln did not have a chassis. Its steering and **suspension** parts were attached to its strong body.

Although few cars were sold during the 1930s, the Zephyr is remembered as one of the most stylish cars of its era.

1936

The Zephyr goes on sale two years after it was first seen at the Chicago World Fair.

1940

Production reaches more than 20,000 cars a year. The company drops the four-door, but introduces a bigger, more powerful version of the Zephyr with a V-12 engine.

The Zephyr was popular, and it saved the company. Ford later took the company over.

Lincoln still exists today, making famous luxury cars such as the Town Car and stretch limousines.

During the 1930s, luxury car makers in the United States were struggling to sell cars. The economy was slow and people did not have the money to spend on big, powerful cars. To save the company, Lincoln introduced the Zephyr as a less expensive model.

Big Seller

It was cheap but also very advanced. The company used a wind tunnel to develop the car's **streamlined** body, just as Chrysler had done with the Airflow.

UNDER THE SKIN

The car makers put the Zephyr's engine in from the top and added its suspension and wheels from below to fit around the single body frame.

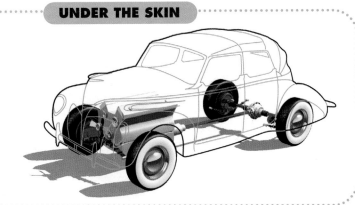

Stutz Bearcat

With its huge engine and racing-car body, the Bearcat was the first true American high-performance car.

The Bearcat had special wheels with wire spokes.

All Bearcats were **right-hand drive** vehicles. The wheel could not go on the left because the engine did not leave room for the steering column there.

The Bearcat did not have doors. The car gave little protection to the driver or passenger.

The car's gearshift and handbrake were fitted on the running board on the driver's side.

The Bearcat's fuel tank was mounted behind the driver's seat.

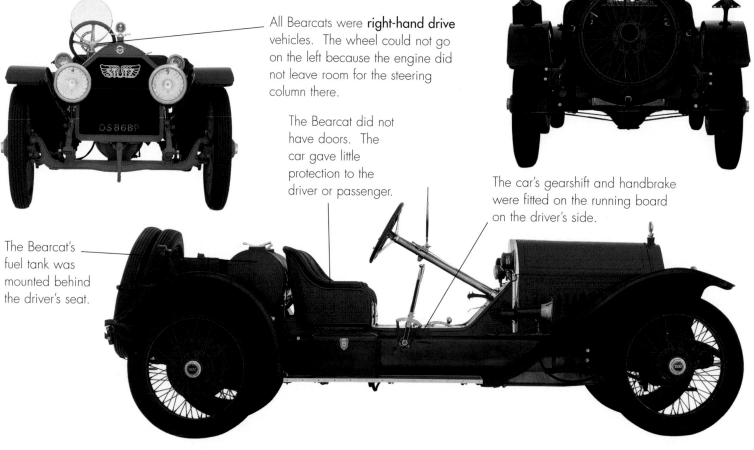

Bearcat drivers had to wear goggles and a hat so that they could drive in such an open car.

1911

Harry Clayton Stutz enters the Indianapolis 500 in a car of his own design and finishes in eleventh place.

1912

Stutz starts building his cars to sell to customers for use on the road.

The Bearcat was first designed as a racing car. Stutz decided, however, to sell Bearcats to wealthy drivers who wanted a really fast car.

Powerful Racer

The Bearcat's 71-horsepower engine does not sound very powerful by modern standards. But it was more powerful than any other car on the road in its day. Its light weight enabled it to go faster than 80 miles (129 km) per hour — more than twice as fast as a Ford Model T.

Driving a Bearcat was a thrill. With no windshield, it felt very fast, indeed. Not surprisingly, its **engine capacity** was huge, at 391 cubic inches (6,407 cc).

UNDER THE SKIN

Stutz wanted to keep the Bearcat as simple as possible, so the car was given hardly any body.

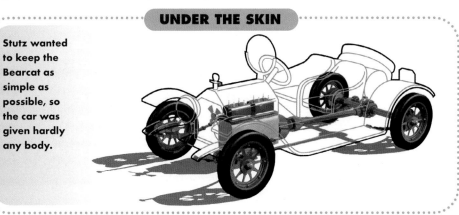

Tucker Torpedo

The Tucker Torpedo was a great design, but it was doomed to failure in spite of its many special features.

Torpedos had three front headlights. The two outer lights did not move, but the center light turned with the steering to light up the road ahead as the driver turned a corner.

Safety was one of the Torpedo's main features. The dashboard was padded, and the steering column folded out of the driver's way in a crash.

The Torpedo's engine was at the back of the car, mounted above the rear axle.

Under the Torpedo's hood was a space that passengers could use to store their bags.

The Torpedo was interesting to look at. It was wider than most cars on the road and also lower.

It is difficult to believe that the Tucker Torpedo was built in the 1940s, because its body shape and styling look much more modern. The Torpedo was a very safe car. It had a third headlight that turned with the steering, a padded dashboard, and a steering column that would collapse in a crash.

New Design

The car was the idea of businessman Preston Tucker. He believed that car design was not moving forward, so he wanted to build a car that would make use of new ideas. He invested all of his money in the project, and the car was popular when it first appeared.

The police later arrested Tucker on charges of fraud. He was cleared of any crime but not before he had gone out of business. Many people believe that other car makers framed him because they feared that the Tucker Torpedo would become successful and threaten their own sales.

MILESTONES

1946

Preston Tucker shows a **prototype** Torpedo for the first time. In 1988, a movie was made about Tucker starring Jeff Bridges (pictured below).

1949

Tucker goes out of business. Only fifty-one Torpedos are ever made.

UNDER THE SKIN

The Torpedo's six-cylinder engine was designed for a helicopter. The company chose it because it was low, flat, and a good fit inside the Torpedo's body.

Willys Knight

The Willys Knight did not look exciting, but it was one of the most solidly built cars of the 1920s.

Some Willys designs were sporty coupes and convertibles, but the company aimed the Knight at more traditional buyers. Its upright design gave more headroom.

Most Knights had wooden spoke wheels. Some buyers ordered disc-type wheels because they looked more stylish.

The Knight's side doors opened in opposite directions like barn doors, making it easy for all the passengers to get in and out.

The Knight's engine had an unusual design called a "sleeve-valve." It was expensive to build, but it was very quiet when running.

The Knight was a sturdy car that was built to last.

1914

Willys opens a new factory in Elyria, Ohio, to build all of its Knights. At first, sales of the Knight are slow because of its price.

1926

Willys introduces a six-cylinder Knight for the last six years the model was made.

The Willys Knight was a well-built and popular car. Its engine had special supports to keep it from shaking. This made the Knight one of the quietest sedans on the road.

It stayed in production for an impressive eighteen years, from 1914 to 1932.

People Carrier

The car's upright body had lots of space inside. It could carry eight people in comfort. Apart from its special engine, the Knight was a simple design with a chassis that was separate from the body, rear wheel drive, and brakes that were operated by cables.

UNDER THE SKIN

The Knight's engine was very tall. The car's hood had to be high for the engine to fit in the car.

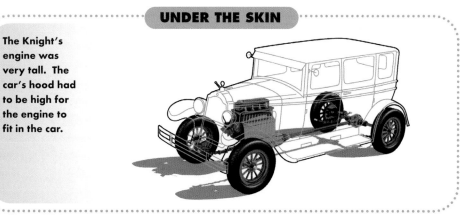

Glossary

aerodynamic having a smooth, sleek surface around which air easily flows

axle a pin or shaft connecting a pair of wheels

capacity the amount of space inside something

chassis the part of a car body to which the engine, transmission, and suspension are attached

convertible a car with a top that can be lowered or removed

coupe a two-door car, usually seating only two people

cylinder a chamber inside an engine where a piston is forced up and down by burning gas to create power

drum brakes brakes that work by pressing against the inside of the wheel to slow the car down

engine capacity the amount of space, or volume, inside the cylinders of an engine; the greater the volume, the bigger the engine capacity and, usually, the greater the engine's power

front-wheel drive a system that sends a car's power from its engine to its front wheels

grille a guard that lets in air to cool the engine's radiator

horsepower a unit of measure of the power of an engine

hot rods cars modified for extra speed

prototype a first test model

rear-wheel drive a system that sends a car's power from its engine to its rear wheels

right-hand drive having the steering wheel on the front, right-hand side

sedans closed automobiles that have two or four doors and a front and rear seat

streamlined designed so that air (or fluid) flows over a surface smoothly and easily

supercars special cars designed to be bigger, faster, and better than ordinary cars

supercharger a pump that forces extra air into an engine to increase power

suspension a system of springs that keeps a vehicle even on bumpy surfaces

transmission a system in a vehicle that controls its gears, sending power from the engine to the wheels to make them move

V-8, V-12 engines that have cylinders placed opposite each other in a V-shape; a V-8 has eight cylinders; and a V-12 has twelve cylinders

wind resistance the force made by still air that slows something moving through it

wind tunnel a room in which colored smoke is blown at a car, showing how smoothly the air passes over its body

For More Information

Books

Big Book of Cars. (DK Publishing)

Car. DK Eyewitness (series). Richard Sutton and Elizabeth Baquedano (DK Children)

Cars. All About (series). Peter Harrison (Southwater)

Cars. Speed! (series). Jenifer Corr Morse (Blackbirch Press)

The Story of Model T Fords. Classic Cars: An Imagination Library (series). David K. Wright (Gareth Stevens Publishing)

Web Sites

Greatest Engineering Achievements of the 20th Century
— Automobile
www.greatachievements.org

Museum of Automobile History
www.themuseumofautomobilehistory.com

Smithsonian Institute — Early Cars: Fact Sheet for Children
www.si.edu/RESOURCE/FAQ/nmah/earlycars.htm

Vintage Sportcar Club of America
www.vscca.org

Publishers note to educators and parents:
Our editors have carefully reviewed these Web sites to ensure that they are suitable for children. Many Web sites change frequently, however, and we cannot guarantee that a site's future contents will continue to meet our high standards of quality and educational value. Be advised that children should be closely supervised whenever they access the Internet.

Index